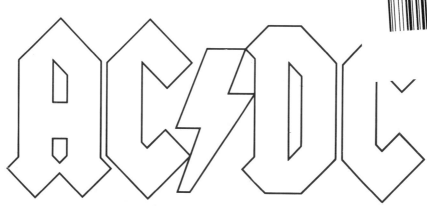

BACK IN BLACK

TRANSCRIPTIONS BY RALPH AGRESTA
EDITED BY ASKOLD BUK

MUSIC SALES CORPORATION
257 PARK AVENUE SOUTH, NEW YORK, NY 10010 USA
MUSIC SALES LIMITED
8/9 FRITH STREET, LONDON W1V 5TZ ENGLAND
MUSIC SALES PTY. LIMITED
120 ROTHSCHILD STREET, ROSEBERY, SYDNEY, NSW 2018, AUSTRALIA

ORDER NO. AM 83056
INTERNATIONAL STANDARD BOOK NUMBER: 0.8256.1305.1

PRINTED IN THE UNITED STATES OF AMERICA BY
VICKS LITHOGRAPH AND PRINTING CORPORATION

AMSCO PUBLICATIONS
NEW YORK/LONDON/SYDNEY

LEGEND OF MUSICAL SYMBOLS

ANGUS YOUNG

BRIAN JOHNSON  CLIFF WILLIAMS

PHIL RUDD   MALCOLM YOUNG

BACK IN BLACK

ANGUS YOUNG, MALCOLM YOUNG, BRIAN JOHNSON

©

back,   yes I'm back._   Well I'm back,   yes I'm

Rhythm figure 2

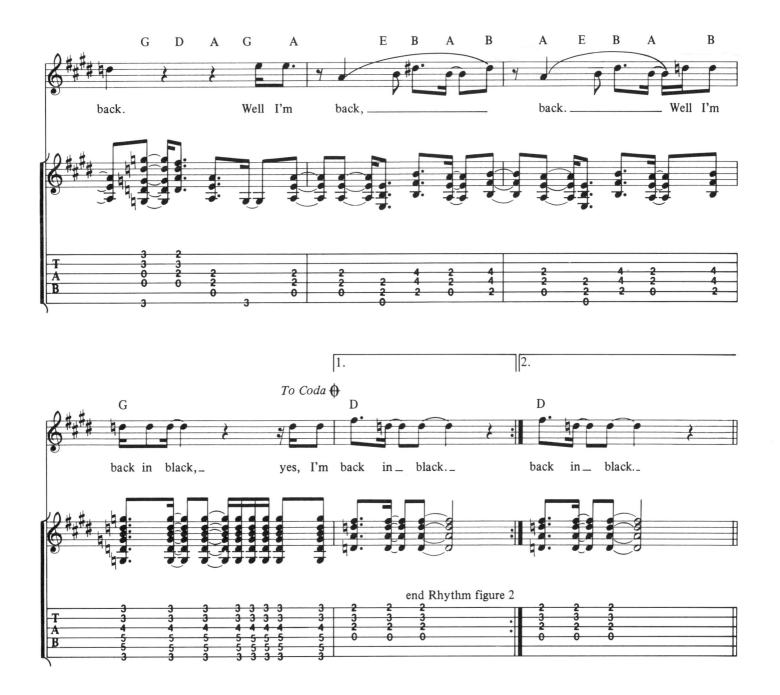

back.   Well I'm   back,_____   back._____ Well I'm

1.   2.

To Coda ⊕   D   D
G   D

back in black,_   yes, I'm back in_ black._   back in_ black._

end Rhythm figure 2

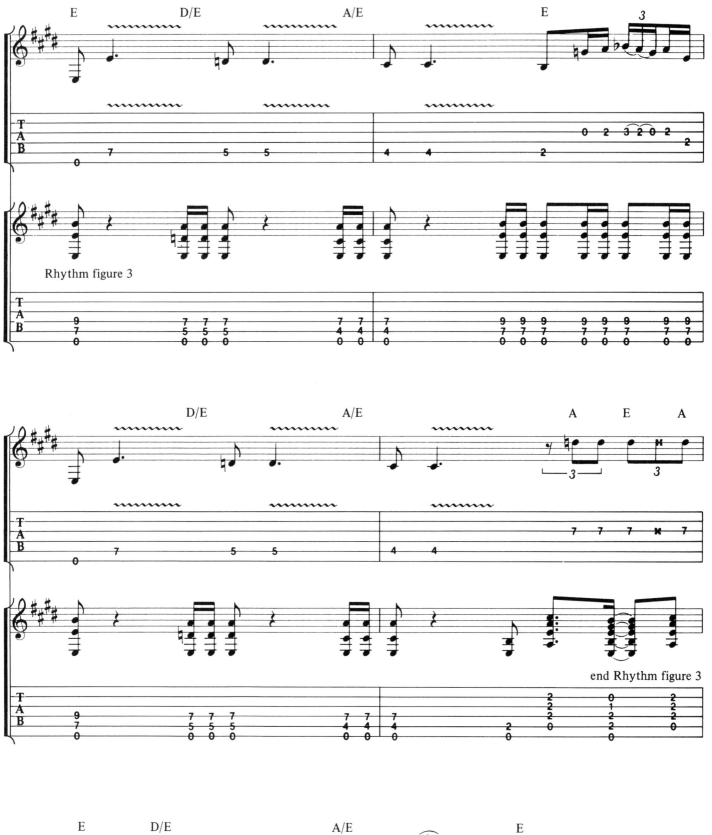

Rhythm figure 3

end Rhythm figure 3

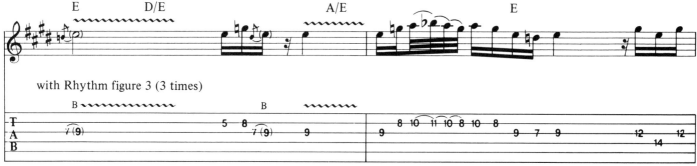

with Rhythm figure 3 (3 times)

Well I'm

Coda

back in black.

Well I'm back _____ back _____

with Rhythm figure 2

Additional Lyrics

2. Back in the back of a Cadillac
   Number one with a bullet, I'm a power pack.
   Yes, I'm in a bang with the gang,
   They gotta catch me if they want me to hang.
   'Cause I'm back on the track, and I'm beatin' the flack
   Nobody's gonna get me on another rap.
   So, look at me now, I'm just makin' my play
   Don't try to push your luck, just get outta my way.

GIVEN THE DOG A BONE

ANGUS YOUNG, MALCOLM YOUNG, BRIAN JOHNSON

©

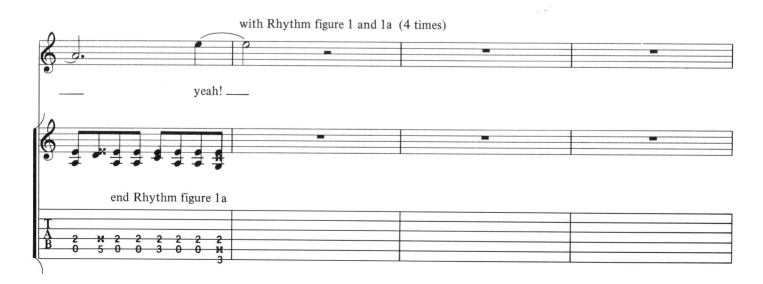

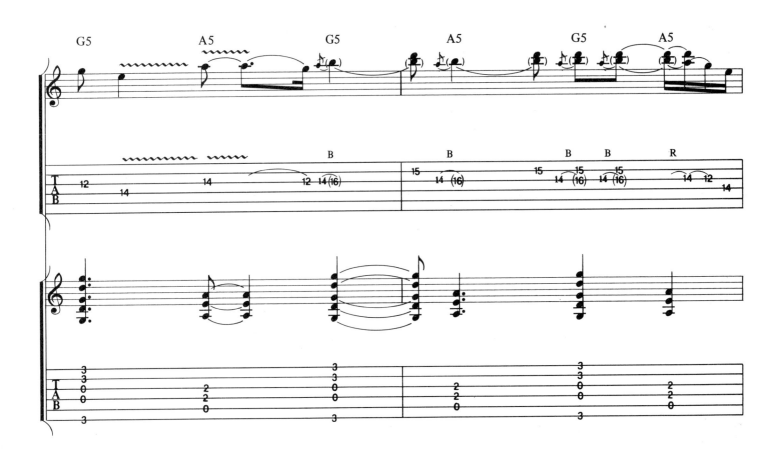

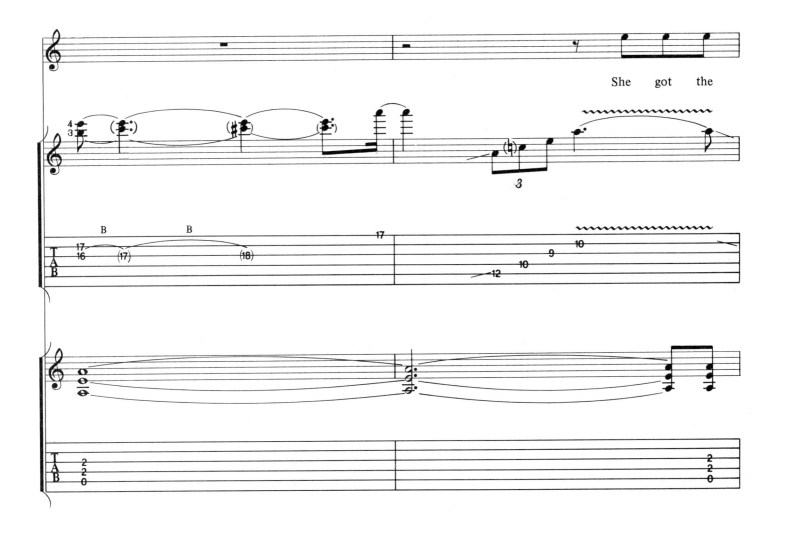

She got the

ROCK AND ROLL AIN'T NOISE POLLUTION

ANGUS YOUNG, MALCOLM YOUNG, BRIAN JOHNSON

©

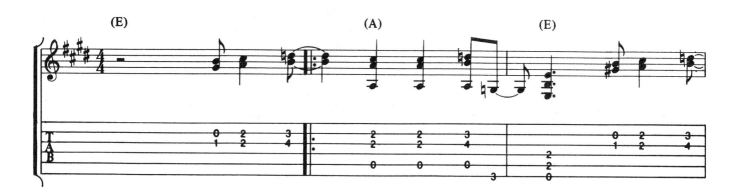

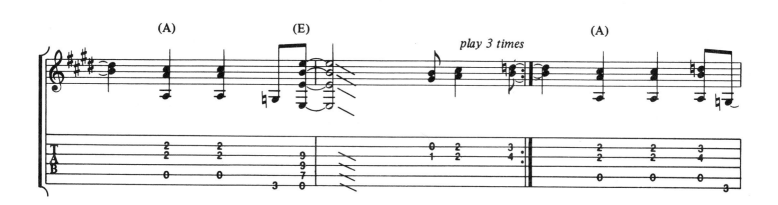

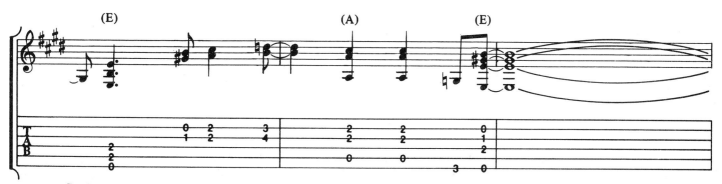

Spoken: Hey, there, all you middle men. Throw away your fancy clothes. And while you're out there sittin' on a fence, so get off your ass and come down here, 'cause rock 'n' roll ain't no riddle, man. To me it makes good, good sense.

Rhythm figure 1

end Rhythm figure 1

1. Hea-vy de-ci-bels are play-in' on my gui-tar.__ We got vi-bra-tions com-in' up from the floor.__

Rhythm figure 2

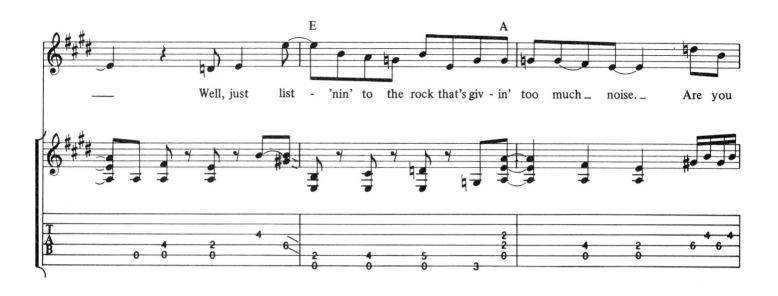

Well, just list - 'nin' to the rock that's giv - in' too much noise. Are you

deaf, you wan - na hear some more. We're just

end Rhythm figure 2

talk - in' a - bout the fu - ture, For - get a - bout the past. It'll

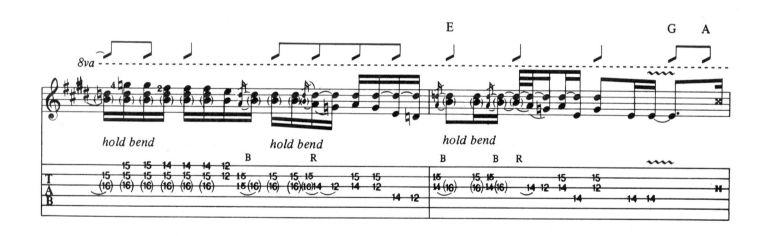

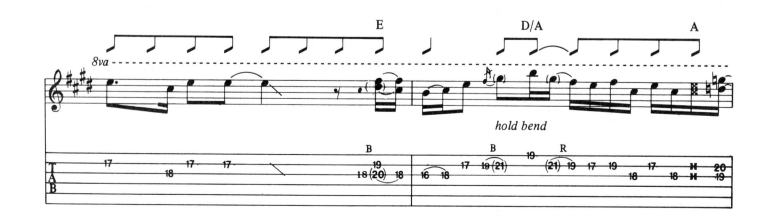

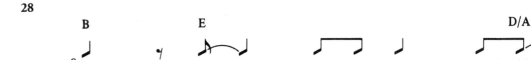

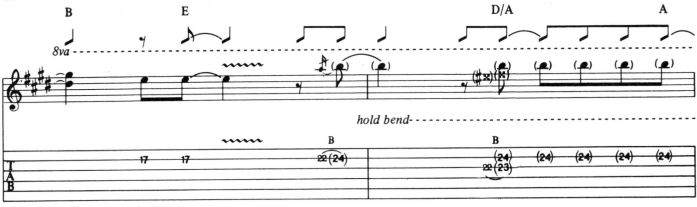

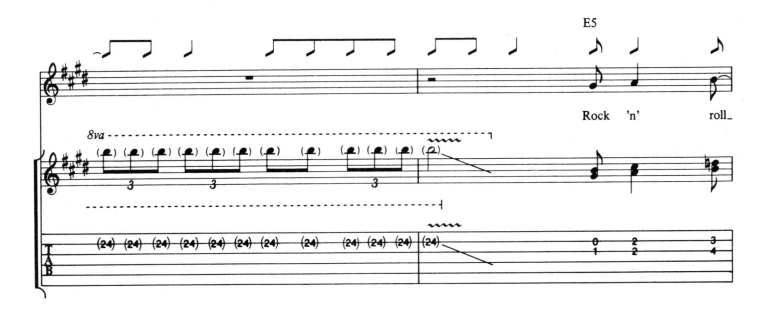

with Rhythm figure 1 (first 4 bars) (3 times)
ad lib guitar solo (16 bars)

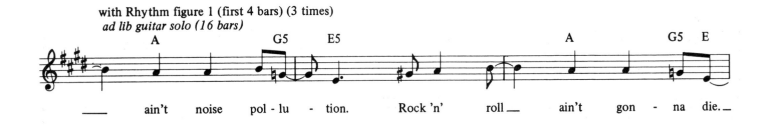

____ ain't noise pol - lu - tion. Rock 'n' roll __ ain't gon - na die. __

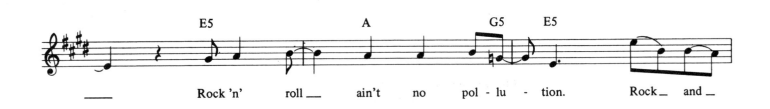

____ Rock 'n' roll __ ain't no pol - lu - tion. Rock __ and __

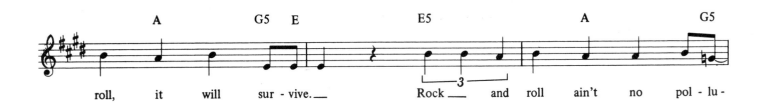

roll, it will sur - vive. __ Rock __ and roll ain't no pol - lu -

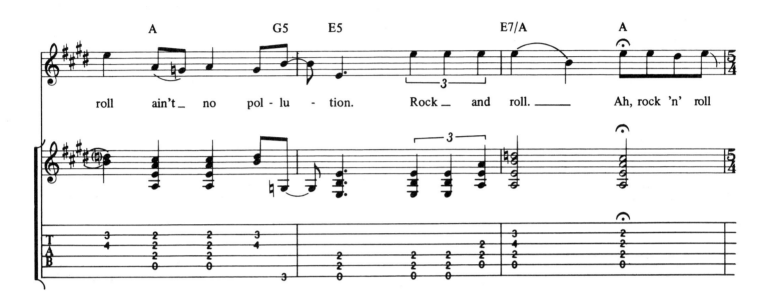

Additional Lyrics

2. I took a look inside your bedroom door,
You looked so good lyin' on your bed.
Well, I asked you if you wanted any rhythm and love,
You said you wanna rock 'n' roll instead.
We're just talkin' about the future,
Forget about the past,
It'll always be with us,
It's never gonna die, never gonna die.

HAVE A DRINK ON ME

ANGUS YOUNG, MALCOLM YOUNG, BRIAN JOHNSON

©

drink on me. _____ Oh, have a

drink on me. _____ Yeah! Oh, have a drink on me. _____

_____ Come on!

Oh!

HELLS BELLS

ANGUS YOUNG, MALCOLM YOUNG, BRIAN JOHNSON

©

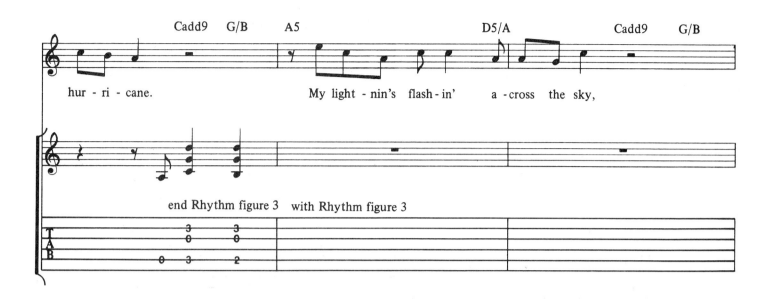

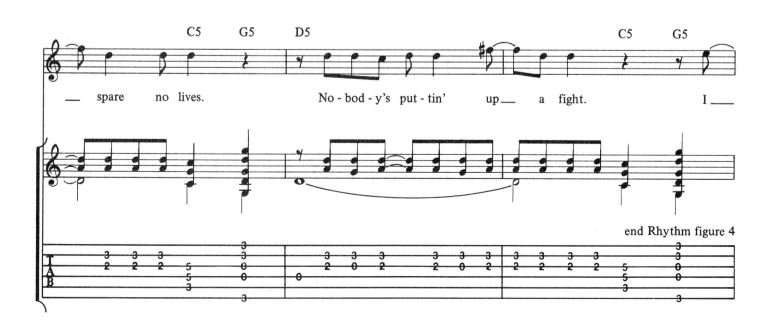

LET ME PUT MY LOVE INTO YOU

ANGUS YOUNG, MALCOLM YOUNG, BRIAN JOHNSON

©
COPYRIGHT © 1980 BY J. ALBERT & SON PTY. LIMITED.
ALL RIGHTS FOR THE U.S. AND CANADA
ADMINISTERED BY J. ALBERT & SON (USA) INC., ASCAP.
INTERNATIONAL COPYRIGHT SECURED. ALL RIGHTS RESERVED. USED BY PERMISSION.

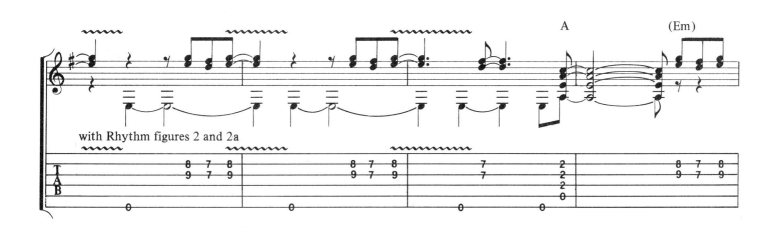

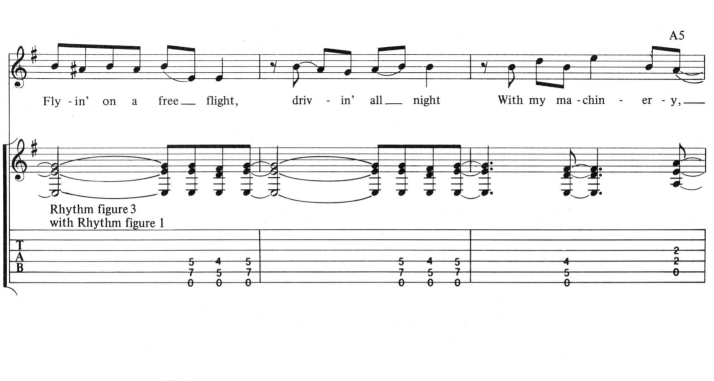

Fly -in' on a free __ flight, driv - in' all __ night With my ma - chin - er - y, __

Rhythm figure 3
with Rhythm figure 1

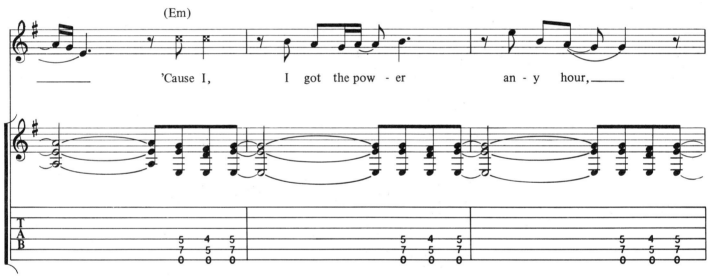

(Em)

__ 'Cause I, I got the pow - er an - y hour, __

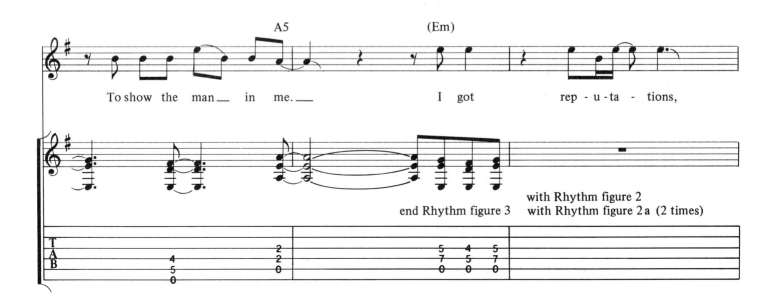

A5   (Em)

To show the man __ in me. __ I got rep - u - ta - tions,

end Rhythm figure 3   with Rhythm figure 2
with Rhythm figure 2 a (2 times)

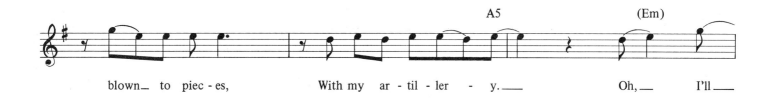

blown__ to piec - es,   With my   ar - til - ler - y.__   Oh, __   I'll__

__ be   guid - in', __   we'll be   rid - in',   Uh, give a   what you got   to   me.__

Rhythm figure 4

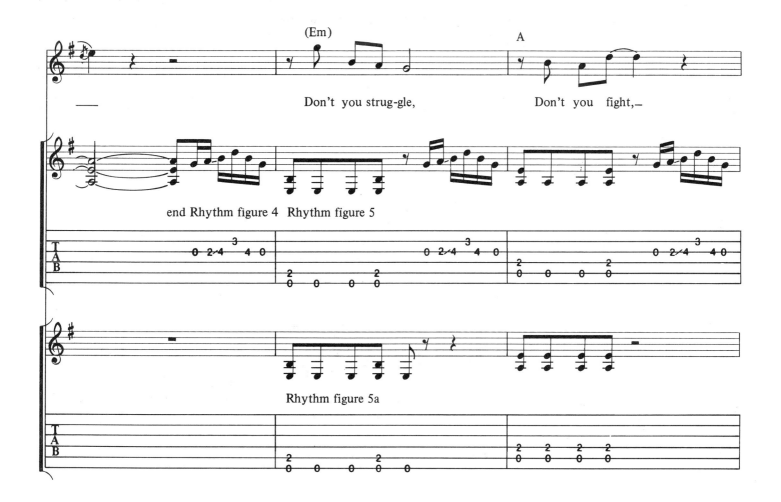

__   Don't you strug-gle,   Don't you fight, __

end Rhythm figure 4   Rhythm figure 5

Rhythm figure 5a

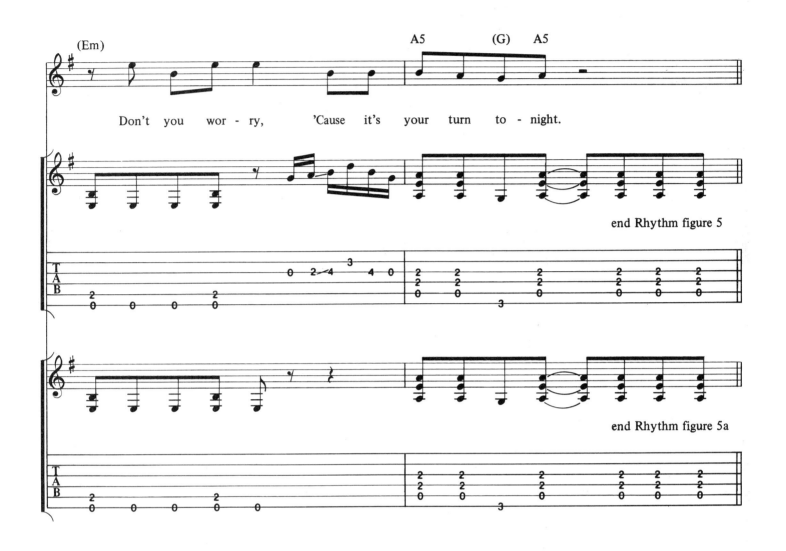

Don't you wor - ry, 'Cause it's your turn to - night.

end Rhythm figure 5

end Rhythm figure 5a

Let me put my love in - to you___ babe,   Let me put my love on the line.___

Rhythm figure 6

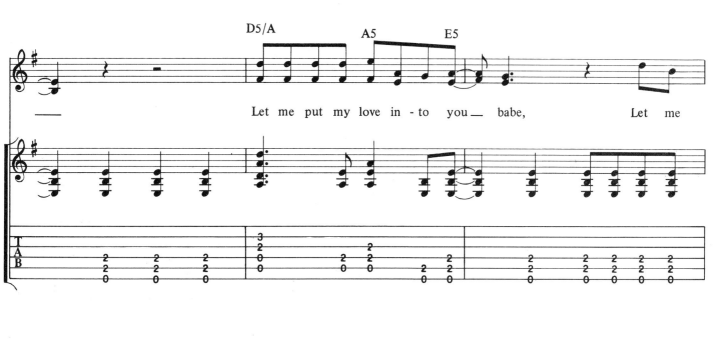

Let me put my love in-to you__ babe, Let me

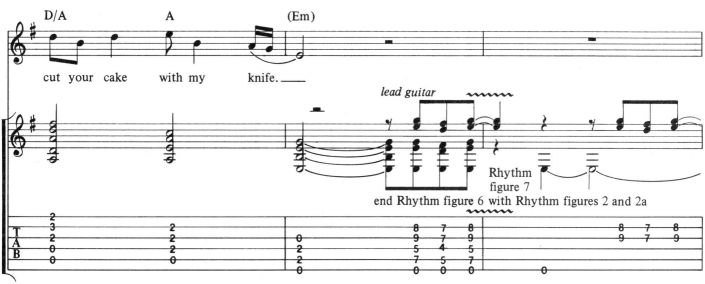

cut your cake with my knife.__

lead guitar

Rhythm figure 7

end Rhythm figure 6 with Rhythm figures 2 and 2a

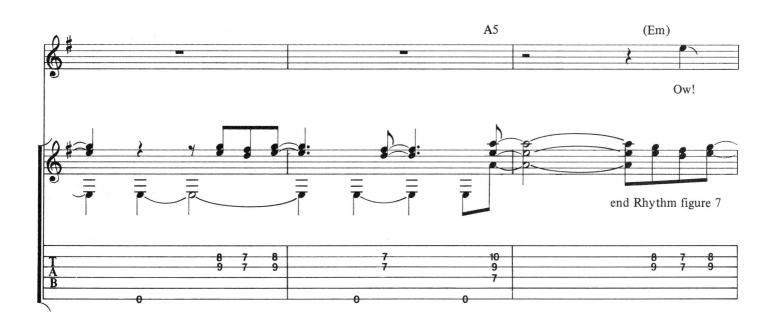

Ow!

end Rhythm figure 7

SHAKE A LEG

ANGUS YOUNG, MALCOLM YOUNG, BRIAN JOHNSON

©

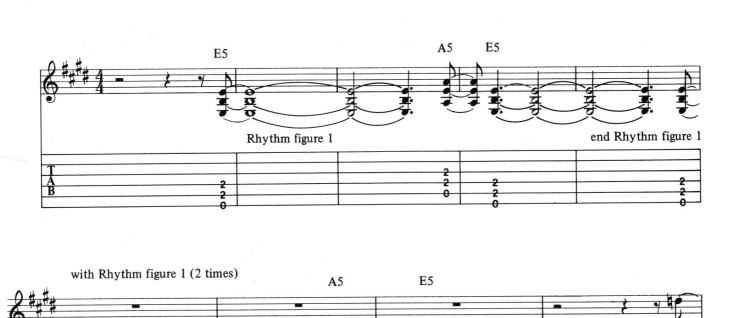

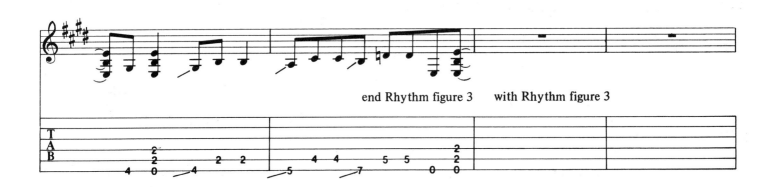

end Rhythm figure 3   with Rhythm figure 3

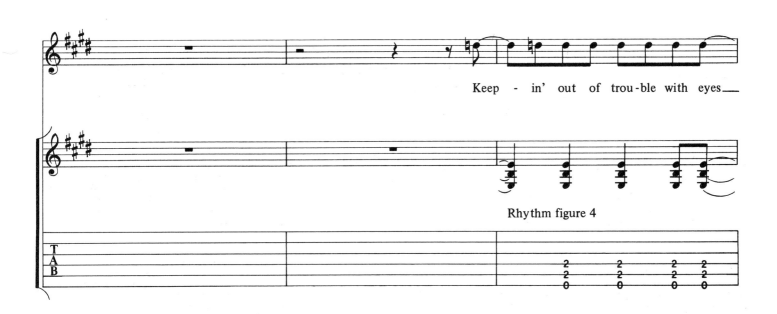

Keep - in' out of trou -ble with eyes____

Rhythm figure 4

____ in the back of my face.   Kick - in' ass____

in the class__ and they tell__ me I'm a damn dis - grace.__

They tell__ me what they think, but they stink, and I real - ly don't

care. Got a mind__ of my own,__ move on,__

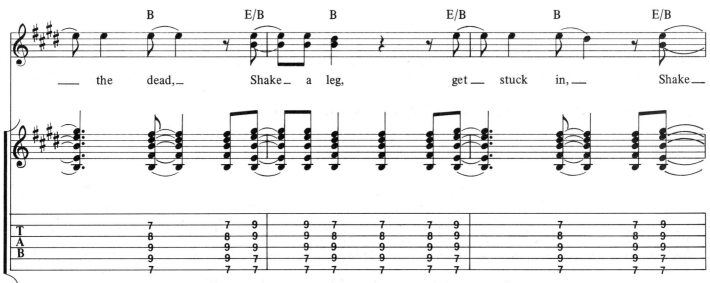

63

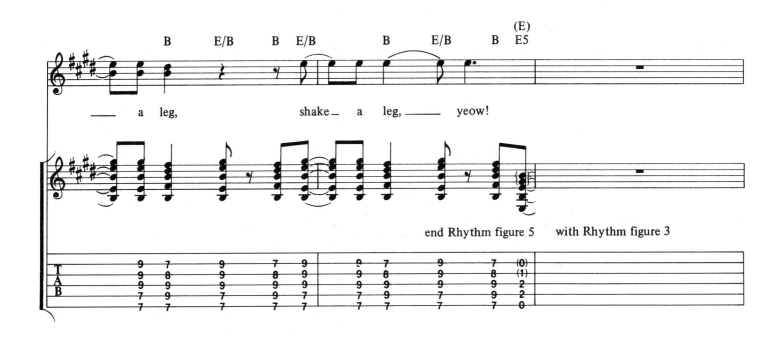

a leg, shake a leg, _____ yeow!

end Rhythm figure 5   with Rhythm figure 3

with Rhythm figure 4

Mag-a-zines,___ wet dreams, dirt-y

wom-en on ma-chines for me.___   Uh, big___

licks, skin flicks, trick-y dicks are my chem-is - try.___

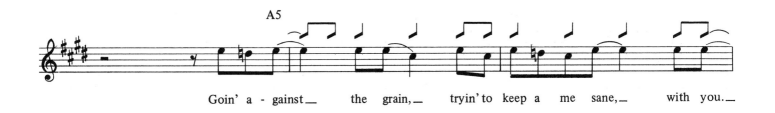

Goin' a-gainst___ the grain,___ tryin' to keep a me sane,___ with you.___

So stop— your— grin-nin' and drop—

— your lin-en for me.— Ah, shake—

with Rhythm figure 5

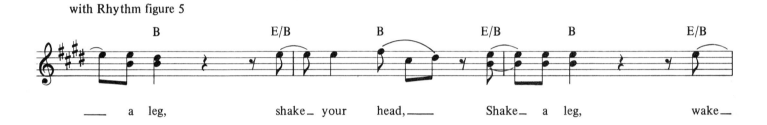

— a leg, shake— your head,— Shake— a leg, wake—

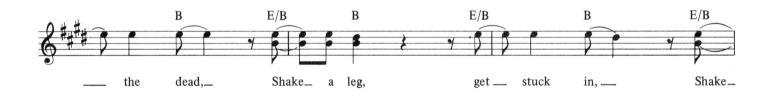

— the dead,— Shake— a leg, get— stuck in, — Shake—

— a leg, shake— a leg.— Yeah!— Shake it!

Come on,— yeah.

Guitar solo

Yo!

A5/C   A5

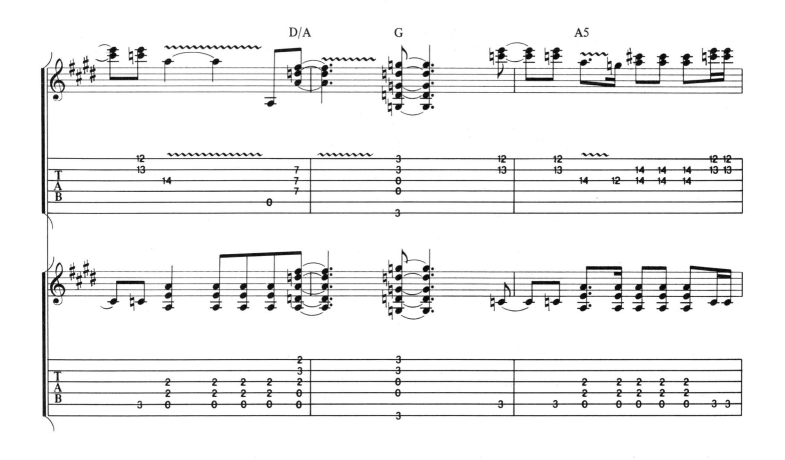

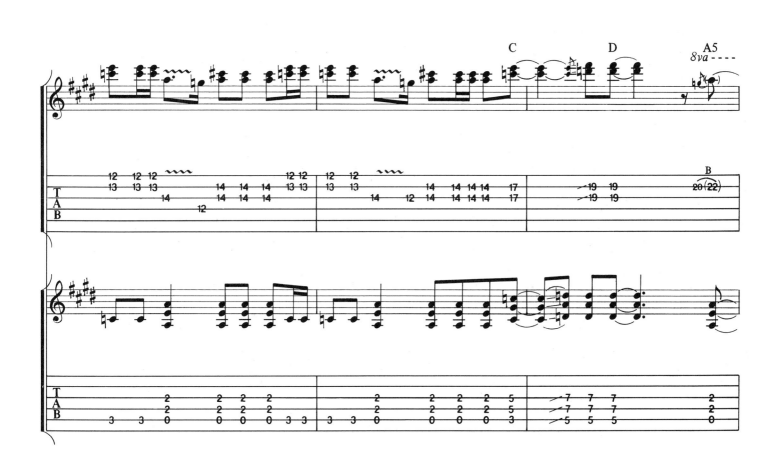

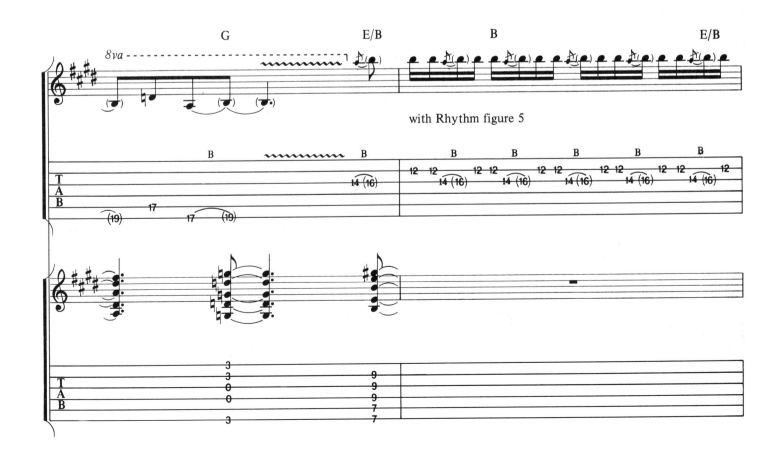

with Rhythm figure 5

WHAT DO YOU DO FOR MONEY HONEY

ANGUS YOUNG, MALCOLM YOUNG, BRIAN JOHNSON

©

What-a ya do for mon-ey hon-ey, How do you get___ your licks? Go!

rhythm guitar

Rhythm figure 6

Guitar solo

end Rhythm figure 6

76

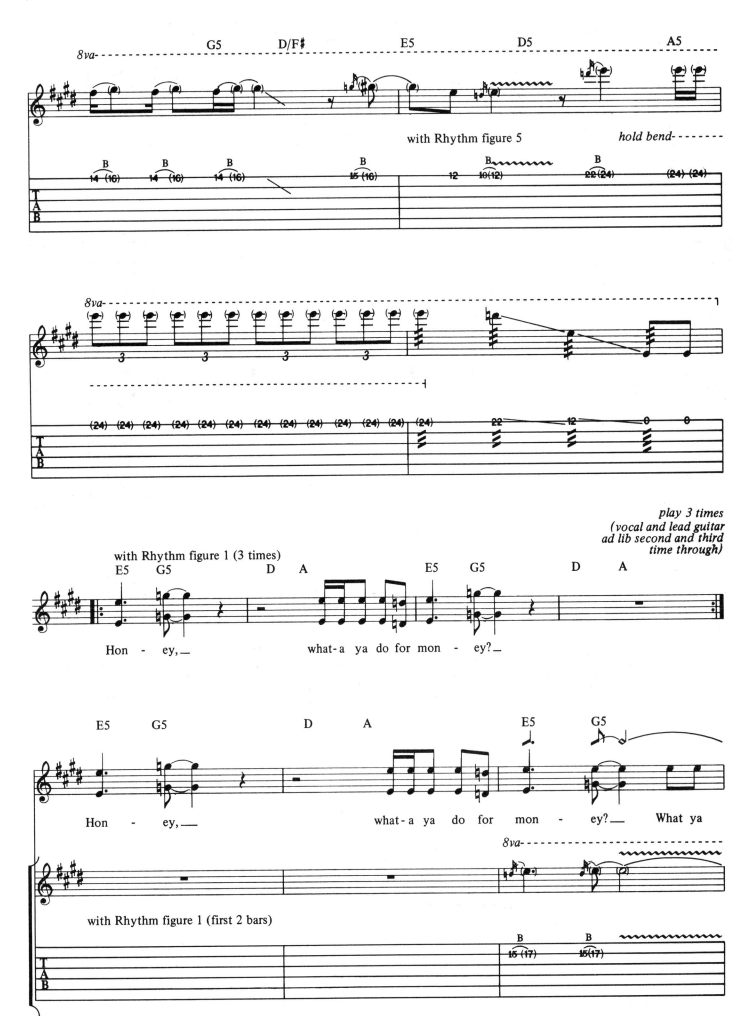

Additional Lyrics

2. You're lovin' on the take, and you're always on the make,
   Squeezin' all the blood outta men.
   They're standin' in a queue, just to spend a night with you;
   It's business as usual again.
   You're always grabbin', stabbin', try'n' to get it back in.
   But girl, you must be gettin' slow,
   So stop your love on the road.
   All your diggin' for gold,
   You make me wonder,
   Yes, I wonder, I wonder.

YOU SHOOK ME ALL NIGHT LONG

ANGUS YOUNG, MALCOLM YOUNG, BRIAN JOHNSON

©

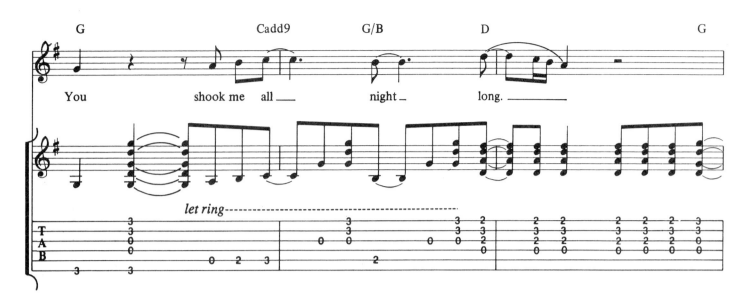

You shook me all __ night __ long. _____

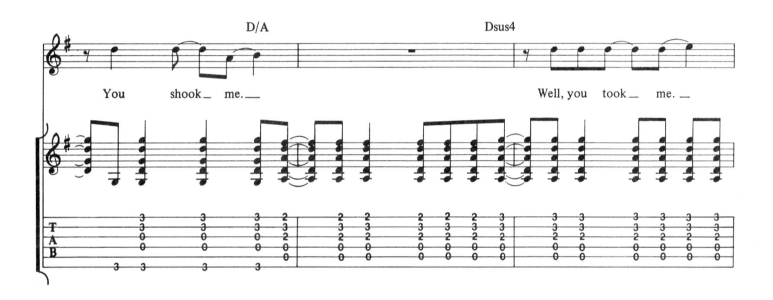

You shook __ me. __ Well, you took __ me. __

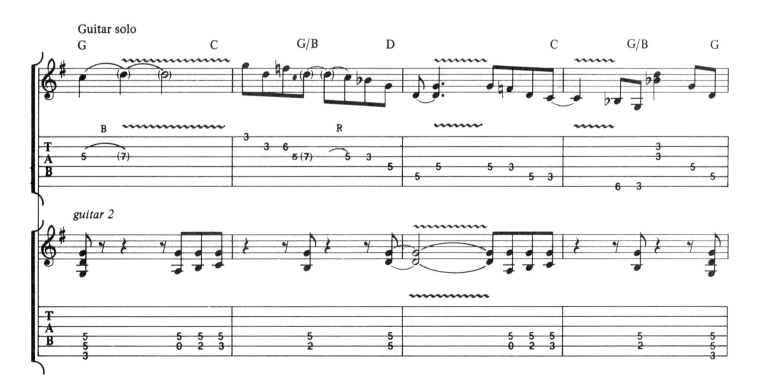

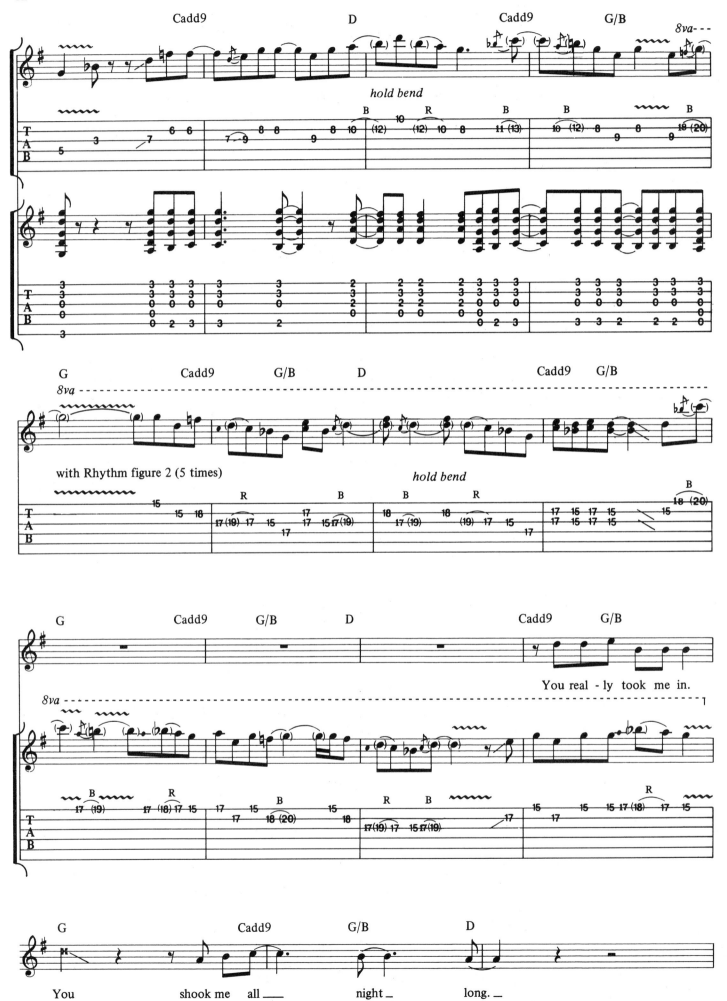

SHOOT TO THRILL

ANGUS YOUNG, MALCOLM YOUNG, BRIAN JOHNSON

©

play to kill; ___ Too man-y wom-en with too man-y pills, ___ yeah.

end Rhythm figure 3

with Rhythm figure 3

Shoot to thrill, ___ play to kill; ___ I got my

gun and I'm read-y, gon-na fire at will, ___ yeah! ___

1.

2.

2. I'm like e- Shoot to thrill, ___ and I'm

with Rhythm figure 3

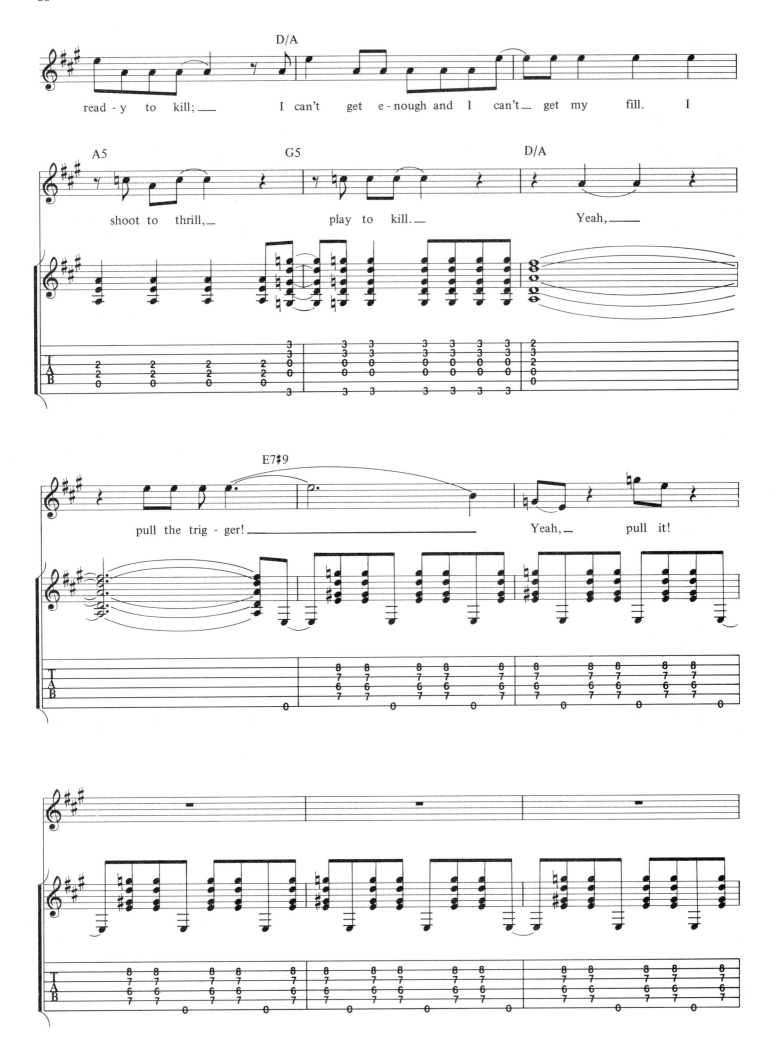

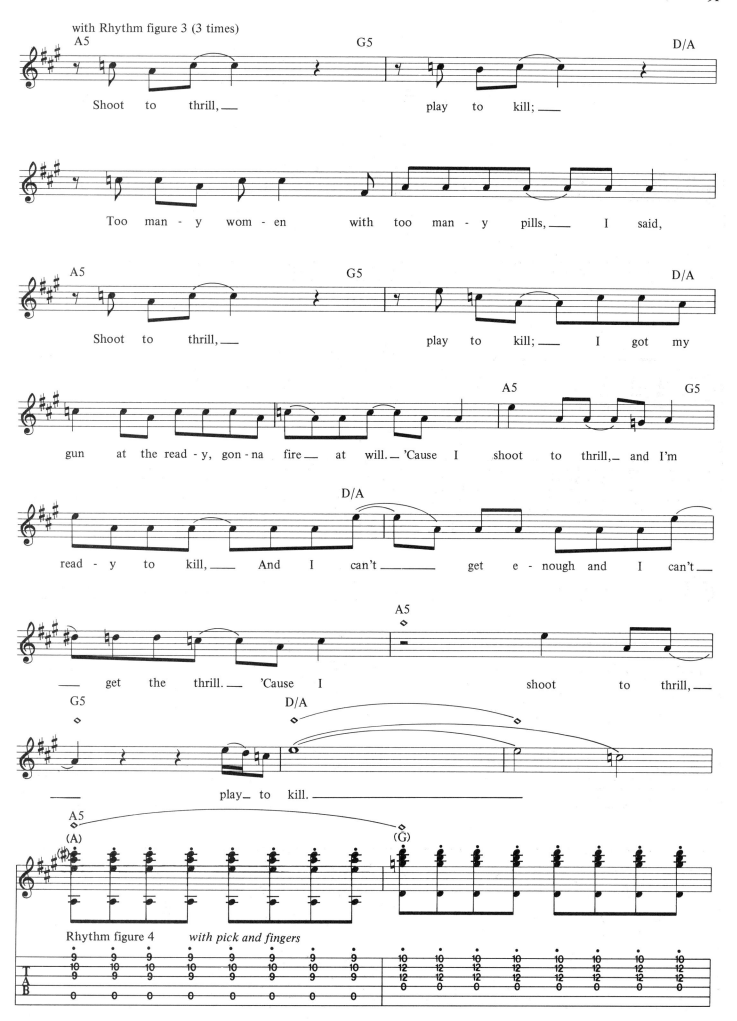

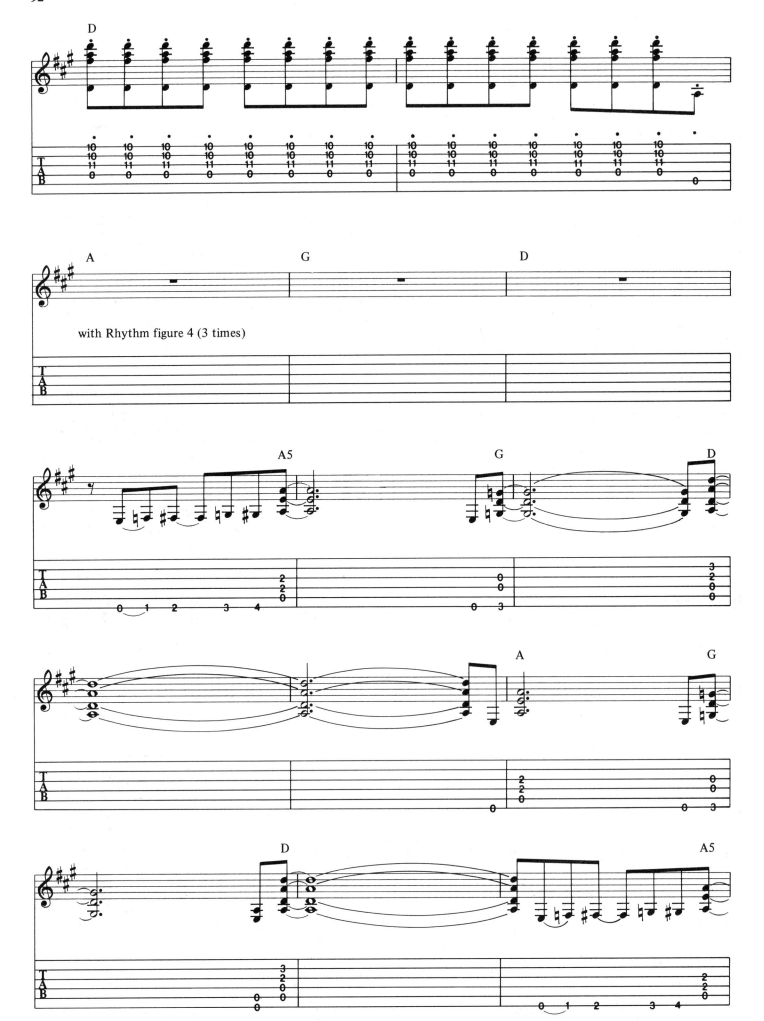

with Rhythm figure 4 (3 times)

Additional Lyrics

2. I'm like evil; I get under your skin,
   Just like a bomb that's ready to blow.
   'Cause I'm illegal; I got everything
   That all you women might need to know.
   I'm gonna take you down,
   Down, down, down.
   So don't you fool around,
   I'm gonna pull it, pull it, pull the trigger.